THE
MONEY
MENTOR

THE
MONEY
MENTOR

A WOMAN'S GUIDE TO MONEY MASTERY

ANANIAH CLARK

BlackaWare Publishing, LLC
Charlotte, North Carolina

THE MONEY MENTOR
A Woman's Guide to Money Mastery
© 2025 Ananiah Clark

BlackaWare Publishing, LLC
4833 Berewick Town Center Drive
Suite E, PMB 134
Charlotte, NC 28273
www.blackawarepublishing.com

Cover design by Ananiah Clark
Interior book design by Ian Koviak
Published by BlackaWare Publishing 07/7/2025
Library of Congress Control Number: 2025910457
ISBN: Paperback: 979-8-9989891-1-7
ISBN: ePub: 979-8-9989891-0-0

All rights reserved. No part of this publication may be reproduced, distributed, or transmitted in any form or by any means, including photocopying, recording, or other electronic or mechanical methods, without the prior written permission of the publisher or author, except in the use of brief quotations embodied in critical reviews and certain other noncommercial uses permitted by copyright laws.

Although every precaution has been taken to verify the accuracy of the information contained herein, the author and publisher assume no responsibility for any errors or omissions. No liability is assumed for damages that may result from the use of information contained within.
Printed in the United States of America on acid-free paper

Because of the dynamic nature of the Internet, any web addresses or links contained in this book may have changed since publication and may no longer be valid.

CONTENTS

Introduction 1

CHAPTER ONE: The Illusion of Success 7

CHAPTER TWO: The Cracks Begin to Show 13

CHAPTER THREE: The Pressure for Change Mounts 19

CHAPTER FOUR: The Breaking Point 25

CHAPTER FIVE: A Chance Encounter 33

CHAPTER SIX: Rewiring Your Mindset about Money 41

CHAPTER SEVEN: Paying Yourself First 49

CHAPTER EIGHT: The Power of Self-Control 57

CHAPTER NINE: Strategically Paying Off Debt 63

CHAPTER TEN: The Truth about Budgeting 72

CHAPTER ELEVEN: Spend with a Purpose 77

CHAPTER TWELVE: Save for a Rainy Day 83

CHAPTER THIRTEEN: The Money Multiplier 91

CHAPTER FOURTEEN: The Simple Path to Wealth 97

CHAPTER FIFTEEN: Building Multiple Streams of Income ... 105

CHAPTER SIXTEEN: Producing Income for the Future 111

CHAPTER SEVENTEEN: Money Mastery Reflection 127

About the Author 133

One person
pretends to be rich,
but has nothing;
Another pretends
to be poor, but has
great wealth.

INTRODUCTION

Money is something we all think about—whether we have too little of it, fear of losing it, or worries about how to make more of it. Some people seem to navigate the financial world effortlessly, building wealth and security, while others struggle, living paycheck to paycheck.

What separates wealthy people from those who are struggling?

Is it luck? Is it intelligence? Or is it something else entirely?

THE HIDDEN RULES OF MONEY

Growing up, many of us were taught that success comes from working hard, getting a good job, and earning a steady paycheck. But what happens when that paycheck disappears as soon as it arrives? What happens when expenses pile up, and no matter how hard we work, financial freedom feels out of reach?

The truth is: Money follows certain rules, rules that most people were never taught.

Schools teach us history, math, and science, but rarely do they teach us how to manage, save, or invest money wisely. Indeed, few parents discuss their finances with their children. Without basic knowledge about money, many people struggle, making financial mistakes that trap them in a cycle of debt and stress.

But there's good news: Wealth is not reserved for the lucky few. Anyone—regardless of background, education, or income—can learn to master money. The key is understanding the timeless principles of wealth that have been used for centuries by those who have built lasting financial success.

A DIFFERENT WAY TO LEARN ABOUT MONEY

This book is not a dry financial textbook filled with complicated jargon. Instead, it is a story about an African-American woman facing real-life financial challenges in modern-day America. Through the narrative of her journey, you will learn about the same principles that have helped countless individuals escape financial struggles and build lasting wealth.

In this book, you meet Mayah, a young professional woman who is chasing the American Dream while struggling to make ends meet. After running out of options to solve her financial problems, she encounters Mr. Clark, a retired businessman who has unlocked the secrets to financial freedom and guides her to money mastery.

Mayah's experiences illustrate:

- **How to break the cycle of living paycheck to paycheck.**
- **The difference between needs and wants.**
- **How to budget wisely without feeling deprived.**

- **Why saving and investing are more important than how much you earn.**
- **How to pay off debt strategically.**
- **The importance of an emergency fund.**
- **How to grow your money without taking huge risks.**
- **How to avoid financial traps that keep people poor.**
- **How to build lasting wealth for yourself and your family.**
- **The importance of financial literacy and continuous learning.**

THE FIRST STEP

If you have ever felt overwhelmed by money, unsure where to start, or frustrated by financial struggles, this book is for you.

This book provides relatable financial lessons through real-life struggles. It breaks down complex financial topics into easy-to-follow principles. It offers practical steps, including twelve steps to money mastery, that anyone can apply to their own life, and it shifts your mindset from just earning money to building lasting wealth.

By the end of this book, you should understand money in a way that will empower you to make smarter financial choices in the future.

No matter where you are today, financial freedom is within your reach. You just need the right knowledge and a plan to follow.

The journey begins now. Are you ready to take the first step?

When your perception changes, Your illusion will disappear.

CHAPTER ONE

The Illusion of Success

Mayah Anderson stepped out of her high-rise apartment building into the crisp city air. The streets were already alive with commuters rushing to work, and taxis honking impatiently while weaving through traffic. The fancy coffee cafe down the street from her apartment was overflowing with early risers clutching their lattes as they fueled up for the day. She was a frequent visitor of the cafe, but today she needed to get going.

Her heels clicked against the sidewalk, each step purposefully rehearsed. Looking at her, the world sees a woman who has it all together. Mayah is successful, ambitious, and effortlessly put-together. And for the most part, she plays the success role well.

Mayah handed the valet her ticket while flashing a polite smile as he rushed to retrieve her car. This was one of the many conveniences she told herself was necessary for her busy lifestyle.

It wasn't long before a sleek, black BMW 5 Series pulled up to the curb with its polished surface reflecting the morning light. Mayah smoothed the front of her tailored blazer and slid into the driver's seat with the familiar scent of leather and luxury wrapping around her. This is the same car she had dreamed about back in college when she imagined what life would look like once she had "made it."

She had the job, the salary, and the lifestyle.

So why did she feel like she was barely keeping up financially?

Her phone buzzed on the passenger seat. A text notification flashed across the screen:

"Your bank account balance: $142.76."

Her stomach clenched. She let out a slow breath, forcing herself to stay calm as she swiped away the message.

She knew better than to check her finances first thing in the morning as it set the wrong tone for the day.

She said to herself, "Ignore it. Push forward." But before she could follow that advice, another notification appeared:

"Credit card payment balance: $8,732. Minimum due: $450."

Now her chest tightened. Another month, another large payment. She had been meaning to pay down this debt.

She kept promising herself it would be paid the next month, but the next month always turned into the month after that, and the balance continued to grow.

Her hands gripped the steering wheel, nails pressing into the leather.

How did this happen?

She had done everything right.

Hadn't she?

This is what she said to herself, clinging to her illusion of reality.

Mayah had always been ambitious. She had graduated near the top of her class, landed a job at a well-respected marketing firm, and quickly climbed the corporate ladder. She worked long hours, attended networking events, and never missed an opportunity to impress the right people.

Her salary had nearly doubled in the past five years to $85,000, which really was more than enough to be financially solvent.

And yet, every month, she felt like she was running on a treadmill set to full speed and never actually getting ahead. Her paycheck would hit her account, and within days, it would be spent.

She tried to push away these thoughts as she merged her car onto the freeway, but they clung to her like a heavy coat.

Where was her money going?

She knew the answer, even if she didn't want to admit it.

- **The $2,500-a-month apartment with floor-to-ceiling windows and a view of the city skyline made her feel important.**
- **The $700-a-month car lease, the after-work drinks, the shopping trips, and the weekend getaways to Miami or New York were all justified as "investments" in her image because, in her mind, she deserved to live a little, and besides, these were just the rewards of success.**

None of the spending felt excessive in the moment. This was just what successful people did with their money.

She had never questioned her lifestyle. Until now.

The "low gas" light on her dashboard flickered on.

Mayah exhaled sharply. She needed to stop for gas, but the thought of watching another $60 drain from her account made her head hurt.

A year ago, she wouldn't have thought twice about it. But today? Today, she was counting every dollar because, for the first time, she was starting to wonder whether she was actually successful or just really good at appearing so.

She didn't know it yet, but this feeling, this slow-creeping realization of the truth was just the beginning.

Her financial reality was about to hit her harder than she ever expected. And soon, she would have no choice but to face it.

Acknowledging the problem is
The first step to
solving the problem.

CHAPTER TWO

The Cracks Begin to Show

Mayah walked into the office lobby, greeted by the familiar scent of fresh coffee and polished marble. The sleek glass doors reflected the image she had carefully presented as professional, confident, and successful. But beneath the surface, the cracks were beginning to show.

She took the elevator to the 14th floor, where the hum of ringing phones and low continuous conversations filled the open floor concept in the neighborhood-like workspace. She passed her co-workers, flashing her usual easygoing smile, but internally, the morning's bank notification still troubled her.

Settling into her desk, she powered on her laptop, trying to block out her disturbing thoughts. She told herself to focus on work. But before she could even check her emails, another reminder popped up on her phone:

"Rent payment due tomorrow: $2,500."

Her stomach clenched. She had just enough to cover it, but barely. After that, her account would be dangerously low until her next paycheck.

She asked herself, "How does this keep happening?"

She glanced at her co-workers, all seemingly unbothered by financial worries. They talked about their weekend plans. Mayah normally joined in the conversation, but today, she felt the weight of something she couldn't quite define.

ACKNOWLEDGING THE PROBLEM

A few hours into the workday, Mayah felt the afternoon slump creeping in. Normally, this was her excuse to grab a latte from the café downstairs—$6.00 wasn't a big deal, right?

But today, she hesitated.

She pulled up her banking app again, staring at the $142.76 balance. It was a small moment, but it felt...different.

Instead of heading to the café, she poured herself a cup of the bitter office-brewed coffee. It wasn't much, but skipping the expense of the latte felt like a tiny, reluctant admission that maybe she needed to start making changes.

By 5:00 p.m., the office chatter turned to after-work drinks. "Mayah, you in?" her co-worker Lydiah asked. "We're hitting that rooftop bar near the river."

This was routine. A way to unwind, network, and stay visible in the company's social scene. Normally, she'd say "yes" without a second thought.

But now, all she could think about was her low bank balance.

She forced a smile. "Maybe next time. Got some stuff to take care of tonight."

Lydiah gave her a curious glance but didn't press her. As the group left, Mayah felt an unexpected twinge of relief. She had just saved at least $50 on drinks and appetizers. But at the same time, she hated that she had to think about it at all.

Was this what financial stress felt like?

She had never considered herself "bad with money." Yet here she was, for the first time in her life, realizing that the lifestyle she had built wasn't actually hers, it was rented—funded by credit cards and a paycheck that vanished too quickly.

She took a deep breath and exhaled while gathering her things.

She wasn't in crisis—yet. But something had to change.

She just didn't know where to start, but at least she was acknowledging the problem.

Change is necessary for growth.

CHAPTER THREE

The Pressure for Change Mounts

Mayah pulled into the parking garage of her apartment building, easing her car into the reserved spot between a sleek Mercedes and a matte-black Tesla. She took a deep breath before exiting the car.

Her apartment was beautiful with floor-to-ceiling windows, a skyline view, and modern finishes. It was exactly the kind of place she had always imagined living in as a symbol of her success.

But standing in the elevator on the way up to the 27th floor, she didn't feel successful.

She felt trapped. Indeed, she was trapped by a:

- **Rent that devoured a third of her paycheck.**
- **Car payment that made her wince every time it was auto-deducted from her bank account.**
- **Lifestyle that felt impossible to maintain, but too terrifying to let go of.**

Her heels echoed against the hardwood floor as she stepped inside, dropping her bag by the door. The silence of the apartment felt heavier tonight.

She tossed her keys onto the counter, noticing a stack of unopened mail. She already knew what was inside the envelopes: bills, account statements, reminders of overdue payments.

Still, reluctantly, she picked up the envelopes and flipped through them.

- **Electric bill: $210.36**

- **Credit card statement balance: $8,732.87**

- **Student loan payment reminder**

She let out a humorless laugh. Oh, right, the student loans monthly bill she had been paying for years, yet somehow, the balance never seemed to shrink. She tossed aside the stack of mail and slumped onto the couch, rubbing her temples.

She wasn't behind on anything yet. But she was cutting it close every month, and it was starting to wear her down.

REALITY HITS AT THE GROCERY STORE

The next evening, Mayah stopped at Whole Foods after work. She used to love grocery shopping there because she could fill her cart with organic produce, imported cheeses, and the occasional bottle of wine without thinking twice about the cost.

But today, as she walked through the aisles, a different feeling crept in.

For the first time, she found herself checking prices.

She picked up a container of pre-cut fruit, but when she saw the price, she hesitated. $7.99 for some pineapple chunks? She put back the container.

The small decisions started piling up:

- **Organic salad mix? Back on the shelf.**
- **Fancy oat milk? Swapped for store brand.**
- **Bottle of wine? Not this time.**

By the time she reached the self-checkout registers, her stomach was tight. She swiped her card and watched the total climb to $74.32.

Not bad, but as her card processed, a wave of frustration hit her.

Was this really what her life had come to?

Second-guessing groceries? Stressing over an $8 fruit cup?

She had worked too hard for this.

And yet, here she was.

She grabbed her bags and walked out, the weight of her finances pressing down on her shoulders heavier than ever.

Something had to change.

And soon it would. Whether she was ready or not.

You are not broke,
you are over-committed
to things that
don't matter.

CHAPTER FOUR

The Breaking Point

Mayah had spent the entire day trying to ignore the weight she felt in her chest. She had pushed thoughts of her overdue bills, declined payments, and mounting debt to the back of her mind.

But by evening, the weight was impossible to ignore.

She had just stepped into her apartment when her phone buzzed.

> "URGENT: Your rent payment has not been received. Please submit payment immediately to avoid late fees or eviction proceedings."

Her breath caught in her throat.

She had completely forgotten about rent.

She fumbled to open her banking app because her hands was shaking.

> Balance: $34.12.

Her rent was $2,500!

She had nothing.

For the first time, the fear wasn't just hypothetical. This wasn't just an overdraft fee or a declined card.

She was on the verge of losing her apartment.

THE MOMENT OF COLLAPSE

Mayah sank onto her couch, staring at the screen in disbelief and uselessly hoping her bank balance would change.

Tears burned in her eyes. How had she let her finances get this bad?

She had a good job. She made real money. And yet, somehow, she was living paycheck to paycheck, drowning in debt, and unable to even pay for the roof over her head.

The truth was undeniable now.

She had been pretending. Pretending, she was fine. Pretending she could afford this life. Pretending she had control.

But she didn't.

And for the first time, she felt the full weight of what her financial situation meant.

Her chest tightened, her breaths coming short and shallow. Was this what a panic attack felt like?

She buried her face in her hands, a sob escaping before she could stop it.

She was stuck. Completely, terrifyingly stuck.

And she had no idea what to do next.

Mayah had finally hit rock bottom. She could no longer avoid the reality of her financial situation, and the fear of losing her place to live forced her to face the truth.

SEARCHING FOR SOLUTIONS

Mayah wiped away her tears and took a deep breath. She couldn't just sit here crying; she had to do something.

She grabbed her laptop and opened her banking app, searching for any solution.

Solution 1: Shuffling Credit Cards

She had three credit cards:

Card #1: Maxed out: $9,103 balance

Card #2: Maxed out: $8,732 balance

Card #3: Available credit: $320

Her rent was $2,500. Even if she maxed out her last card, it wouldn't be enough.

She considered taking out a cash advance, but the 29.99% interest made her stomach churn.

Still, wasn't that better than being evicted?

She added it to her list of last resorts.

Solution 2: Borrowing Money

Her fingers hovered over her phone. Who could she ask for a loan?

Her parents? No. They had already helped with her student loans years ago. Asking them for money would be humiliating.

Her friends? They all thought she was financially stable. She had spent years keeping up appearances, and she couldn't ruin that now.

A payday loan?

She quickly Googled. "Same-day payday loans."

400% APR.

She slammed her laptop shut.

Absolutely not.

Solution 3: Selling Some Possessions

She glanced around her apartment. What did she own that was worth anything?

Her designer handbags? Maybe she could get a few hundred dollars selling them online.

Her TV, and electronics? Not enough to make a real difference. Her car?

She paused.

Her car was worth $40,000. But she still owed $30,000 on it. Selling it could free up her $700 monthly payment…but how would she get to work?

Her stomach turned as she realized that none of her solutions was enough.

REALITY SETS IN

Mayah pressed her hands to her temples. She was out of options.

She had spent years living in denial, swiping her credit cards and financing a lifestyle she couldn't actually afford.

And now, she was facing the consequences.

She had tried to fix it. She had looked for every way out. But for the first time, she realized this was bigger than her.

She didn't need a temporary fix. She needed a complete reset.

But how? Where should she even start?

Mayah had officially exhausted all of her options. She had tried everything she could think of to solve her financial crisis but now realized that her approach to money is fundamentally broken.

With the right kind of knowledge, you can build the future you want.

CHAPTER FIVE

A Chance Encounter

Mayah sat in her car, gripping the steering wheel. The weight of the last 24 hours pressed down on her with the suffocating reality of her financial situation.

She had failed.

She had tried to fix things, to find a way to stay afloat, but nothing worked. She was drowning.

Her phone buzzed.

> "FINAL NOTICE: Immediate action required on your overdue rent payment."

She shut her eyes. The panic rose again, but this time, it was mixed with something else: a sense of resignation.

She had to do something, anything.

With a deep breath, she started the car and started driving.

A FORTUITOUS MEETING

She had no plan, but she found herself pulling into the parking lot of a small coffee shop a few blocks from her office. It wasn't her usual spot like the sleek, overpriced café she frequented, but a cozy, unassuming place she had passed by a hundred times.

She just needed to breathe.

Inside, the scent of fresh coffee and baked goods filled the air. It was quieter than the chain cafés, with its warm lighting and shelves lined with books.

She ordered a plain black coffee, the cheapest thing on the menu, and sat by the window, staring at her phone.

Her banking app was still open and showing $34.12.

She ran a hand down her face, lost in thought.

"Long day?"

Mayah blinked and looked up.

A man older than she, holding a cup of coffee, stood nearby. He looked to be in his mid-50s, dressed casually but neatly—the kind of person who didn't have to prove anything to anyone.

She forced a tired smile. "Something like that."

He gestured to the empty seat across from her. "Mind if I sit?"

Mayah hesitated, then shrugged. "Go ahead."

He settled in, taking a sip of his coffee. "I've seen that look before."

"What look?"

He set down his cup. "The one people have when they realize they're in over their heads."

Mayah stiffened. She let out a dry laugh, expressing surprise, and then said, "That obvious?"

"I've been there myself," he said with an empathetic smile.

She studied him; something about his calm presence was both comforting and frustrating.

"Let me guess," she said. "You got through it, figured everything out, and now you're going to tell me it's all going to be fine?"

His smile widened. "Not exactly. But I can tell you this, it won't get better by doing the same things that got you here."

Mayah exhaled, shaking her head. "I don't even know where to start."

He leaned back, sipping his coffee. "Well...maybe that's where I can help."

My name is Mr. Clark.

Mayah carefully eyed him while stirring her coffee, even though she had no intention of drinking it. My name is Mayah. "You think you can help me?" she asked, her tone edged with doubt.

Mr. Clark replied, "I think I can point you in the right direction. But whether you listen? That's up to you."

Mayah exhaled, shaking her head. "No offense, but I don't even know you. Why should I take financial advice from some random guy in a coffee shop?"

"Fair question. You shouldn't. At least, not yet."

Mayah expected some sales pitch, some offer to fix her life for a price. But Mr. Clark just sipped his coffee, completely unfazed.

"Look," she said, crossing her arms. "I've read the blogs and watched the videos on YouTube. I've tried budgeting, cutting back on expenses, all of it. It doesn't work. No matter what I do, I can't get ahead."

Mr. Clark listened intently, as if he had heard this before. "So, what's your plan now?"

Mayah hesitated. "I, I don't know."

"Exactly." Mr. Clark set down his cup and said, "That's the real problem. You don't have a plan. You've been reacting to your money, not controlling it."

Mayah frowned. "I make good money. I should be fine."

"Should be," Mr. Clark echoed. "But you're not."

Mayah clenched her jaw. She didn't need some stranger rubbing it in. "Okay, so what? You think you have the answer?"

Mr. Clark leaned forward slightly. "I think I've been where you are. Making good money, thinking that was enough, until I realized I was running in place. Stressed. Broke. Waiting for my next paycheck just to survive. Like most people, I struggled financially because I did not know the principles of money, or I did not observe them."

Something about his words hit a little too close. Mayah looked away, tapping her nails against her coffee cup.

Mr. Clark continued, "I don't have all the answers, Mayah. But I do know this, you're not stuck because you don't make enough. You're stuck because you don't know how to make your money work for you."

Mayah scoffed. "Yeah? And what does that even mean?"

Mr. Clark smiled. "I guess that depends on whether you actually want to find out."

Mayah was skeptical, but Mr. Clark had planted a seed of doubt in her mind. What if she has been going about her finances all wrong?

SWALLOWING HER PRIDE

The next day, she stood outside of the coffee shop, shifting nervously from foot to foot.

She had spent the night thinking about everything Mr. Clark had said about not having control over her money.

She didn't want to admit it, but she needed help. Real help.

And that meant going back to Mr. Clark.

After taking a deep breath, she pushed open the door to the coffee shop, and there, in the same corner as before, was Mr. Clark.

He was reading a newspaper, his coffee in one hand, looking as calm as ever.

Mayah hesitated, then walked over. "Is this seat taken?"

Mr. Clark looked up, a knowing smile played on his face. "Not at all."

She sat down, fingers fidgeting with the sleeve of her jacket.

"So…my finances are a mess. But you were right, I had no idea just how bad it was."

Mr. Clark just listened.

Mayah took a deep breath while rubbing her temples. "In the past, I tried fixing things. Cut some expenses, made a budget, even asked for a raise at work, but it's still not enough. I feel like I'm just putting out fires while the whole house is still burning down."

Mr. Clark leaned back while studying her. "So, what do you want to do now?"

Mayah hesitated, then met his gaze.

"I want to learn about money," she said quietly. "For real this time."

Mr. Clark, who had helped many people find financial freedom, smiled and replied, "Good, then let's get to work."

He reached into his briefcase and pulled out a new notebook and handed it to Mayah, explaining, "This will be your guide to money mastery."

The first step to money mastery: Developing a mindset to learn
What you do not know.

CHAPTER SIX

Rewiring Your Mindset about Money

Mr. Clark tapped his fingers against his coffee cup, watching Mayah closely. "Before we get into numbers, we need to talk about something more important."

Mayah frowned. "More important than money?"

Mr. Clark smirked. "More important than how you handle it. Your mindset about money is what got you into this mess. And until you change that, no amount of budgeting is going to save you."

Mayah folded her arms. "I already know I need to stop spending so much."

Mr. Clark shook his head. "That's not what I mean. Tell me—when you think about money, what's the first thing that comes to mind?"

Mayah hesitated. "Bills. Stress. Not having enough."

Mr. Clark nodded. "And that's exactly the problem."

SCARCITY VS. ABUNDANCE

Mr. Clark leaned forward. "You've been playing defense your whole life, Mayah. You think about money in terms of survival. Paying bills. Cutting expenses. Stretching your paycheck. And because of that, you always feel like you're running out."

Mayah frowned. "Because I *am* running out."

Mr. Clark smirked again. "Or maybe it's because you only focus on what's leaving, never on what's coming in—or how to grow it."

Mayah blinked. "Wait...what?"

Mr. Clark sat back. "People with a scarcity mindset think money is limited. That there's never enough, and that the only way to stay afloat is to save, cut back, and avoid risk. They focus on what they don't have."

Mayah thought back to all the times she had agonized over small expenses—turning down dinner invites, stressing over grocery prices—while still blowing hundreds on impulse buys.

Mr. Clark continued, "Wealthy people, on the other hand, don't think about money as something to fear. They see it as a tool. Something to be earned, invested, and multiplied. They focus on growth."

Mayah swallowed. "So, you're saying...I need to stop thinking like I'm broke?"

Mr. Clark laughed. "I'm saying you need to start thinking like someone who controls their money, instead of letting it control you."

Mayah nodded slowly. "Okay...so how do I do that?"

Mr. Clark smiled. "First, you stop believing the biggest lie about money."

THE BIGGEST LIE ABOUT MONEY

Mayah leaned in. "Which is?"

Mr. Clark met her gaze. "That making more money will fix your problems."

Mayah stiffened. "Wait, but—"

Mr. Clark held up a hand. "I know you are probably thinking if you made $10K more a year, you'd be fine, right?"

Mayah nodded. "I mean...yeah."

Mr. Clark shook his head. "Then why are people making six figures still broke?"

Mayah opened her mouth, then shut it.

Mr. Clark continued. "Because money problems aren't about how much you make. They're about how you handle what you have. If you can't manage $50K a year, you won't magically know how to manage $100K."

Mayah exhaled. That one hit hard.

She had always believed a raise would fix everything. That once she made just a little more, the stress would go away.

But looking at her own finances, she knew that wasn't true.

She had already received raises before.

And yet, she was still broke.

Mr. Clark leaned forward. "You don't need more money, Mayah. You need a new system."

Mayah took a deep breath. "Okay...so what's the system?"

"Now you're asking the right questions."

THE MONEY SYSTEM

Mr. Clark asked Mayah to take out her notebook and write the following:

"The money system is the foundation of money management that includes creating a budget that works, saving with a purpose, and making every dollar work for you. The money system is a mindset shift from what you had been taught about money to learning what you don't know about money."

Then Mr. Clark added, "Learning what you do not know about money is the first step to money mastery. When you transform your mindset, habits, and relationship with money, you will see that financial freedom isn't about how much money you make; it's about how you manage what you have and the small, consistent steps you take to improve your situation."

Mr. Clark, with a serious look on his face, made eye contact with Mayah and said, "You have the power to change your life, and this is your starting point. The journey ahead will feel challenging at times, but every step you take toward money mastery will bring you closer to your goals."

Mayah still had doubts, fears, and challenges, but she also had a willingness to take small steps toward a better financial future with Mr. Clark as her money mentor.

The second step to money mastery: It's not about how much you make, it's about how much you keep.

CHAPTER SEVEN

Paying Yourself First

Mr. Clark took a sip of his coffee and set it down, then folded his hands on the table. "All right, Mayah. Let's talk about your paycheck."

Mayah exhaled noisily. "What about it? It comes in and then it goes right back out."

Mr. Clark smiled. "Exactly." While stirring his coffee he began, "Now tell me, when you get paid, what's the first thing you do?"

"Well, I pay my bills, then I buy groceries, and whatever is left, I try to enjoy."

"There's the problem," Mr. Clark pointed out. "The moment you get paid, you start paying everyone else first—your landlord, your utilities, your favorite restaurants, your car lender, your credit card company, Netflix, Amazon—but what about you?"

Mayah frowned, "What do you mean? I have to pay my financial obligations to live on my own."

Leaning forward, Mr. Clark asked Mayah, "Whom do you work

for? You work hard every day, right?"

Mayah scoffed. "Obviously."

"But instead of keeping anything for yourself, you give it all away. You've been trained to put your bills, debts, and expenses first, and hope there's something left for you at the end."

Mayah nodded slowly. "Yeah...."

Mr. Clark continued, "And how has that been working out for you?"

"It hasn't!" Mayah let out a dry laugh.

"You are the last person to touch the money you are working hard to earn," Mr. Clark noted. Mayah crossed her arms, but listened intently to what Mr. Clark was saying.

The first step to wealth and money mastery is simple: Pay yourself first.

A NEW WAY TO HANDLE MONEY

The "pay yourself first" strategy is one of the most powerful financial habits you can develop.

Mayah leaned forward. "How do I do that?"

Mr. Clark smiled. "Before you pay a single bill, before you spend a dime, set aside at least 10% of your income for yourself. Treat it like a bill that is non-negotiable. This money isn't for rent, it isn't for fun, and it isn't to make the world rich. It's the foundation of your future wealth."

Mayah said, "But I can barely cover my expenses as it is."

Mr. Clark said, "That's what everyone says, but somehow, people who are serious about following the principles of money find a way to pay their bills. If you take your cut first, you'll adjust your spending to make it work. This mindset shift ensures that your financial future is the priority, not just your monthly expenses. Let me give you an example using your paycheck."

He asked Mayah to open your notebook and write down the amount of money she makes a year.

Mayah wrote $85,000.

Mr. Clark then explained the following:

$85,000 ÷ 12 months = $7,083 (before taxes, which would be 30%)

$7,083 × 30% taxes = $2,124

$7,083 − $2,124 = $4,959 (before pretax deductions such as medical insurance, 401K, etc., which would be $459)

$4,959 − $459 pretax deductions = $4,500 take-home pay per month

HOW TO PAY YOURSELF FIRST IN TWO STEPS

Step 1: Decide on a Percentage or Fixed Amount.

A good starting amount is 10% of your income, but if that's too high, start with 1% or 5%, and increase the amount over time.

If you get paid $4,500 per month, saving 10% means $450 goes into savings before you touch anything else.

Step 2. Automate Your Savings.

Set up an automatic transfer from your checking account to your savings or investment account on payday.

Again, you must treat this like a non-negotiable bill—it's not optional.

Mayah stared at her coffee, taking in all this information. "And if I start doing what you suggest? What happens?"

Mr. Clark smiled and explained, "Your money will finally start working for you instead of disappearing. Give it time, and one day, you won't be worrying about making ends meet, you'll be wondering how to invest what you've saved."

For the first time in a while, Mayah felt a spark of hope. "Okay," she said, "I'll try it."

Good, said Mr. Clark, raising his cup, "Here your first assignment."

Mayah said, "You're giving me homework?"

"Think of it as a challenge. Next paycheck, before you spend a single dollar, I want you to take 10% and move it into a separate savings account."

Mayah swallowed. "And then what?"

"Then you come back and tell me how it felt," Mr. Clark responded.

Mayah stared at the notebook, then at Mr. Clark.

Could she really do this?

Only one way to find out....

The third step to money mastery: Either you control your money or your money will control you.

CHAPTER EIGHT

The Power of Self-Control

Mayah stared at her phone screen with her bank app open. Her paycheck had just hit.

And now, she had to make a choice: Save 10%, which is the amount Mr. Clark told her to save before she did anything else with her money.

She took a deep breath and hovered her finger over the transfer button to send $450 into savings.

She bit her lip. That was a lot of money to move out of reach.

Her rent was due in a few days. Her credit card payment was coming up. What if she needed that money?

The doubt started creeping in.

Maybe Mr. Clark didn't understand how tight things actually were.

Maybe this was a bad idea.

Maybe she should wait until next month, when things weren't so....

No! She exhaled sharply.

These were the same excuses she had been making for years, always waiting until next month to pay down debt.

And somehow, next month never came.

Before she could second-guess herself again, she tapped the transfer button.

Transfer complete.

Her stomach twisted, but she had done it.

Now she had to live with it.

INSTANT REGRET

For the next few days, Mayah couldn't stop checking her account.

Watching her checking balance sit lower than usual made her anxious.

And then, of course, life tested her.

- **Her friend texted about dinner plans: $50 minimum at that riverside restaurant.**
- **She received an email about a sale on those shoes she'd been eyeing: 50% off—limited time.**
- **And then, worst of all—her car battery died and it would be $180 to replace it.**

Mayah groaned. She could easily move the money back from savings. It was right there. And for a moment, she almost did. But then she stopped herself. This was a test.

Mr. Clark never said it would be easy. And if she gave in now, she'd just be repeating her old bad habits about money.

So, instead of pulling the money from savings, she made different choices:

- **She skipped dinner out and invited her friends over instead.**
- **She ignored the sale, and told herself there would always be another one.**
- **She covered (barely) the car battery with what was left in checking.**

It wasn't fun. It wasn't comfortable. But when she checked her savings account at the end of the week, she felt something new: pride, self-control, and a sense of empowerment.

For the first time, she had put herself first.

And she wasn't going back.

The fourth step to money mastery: Break free from debt.

CHAPTER NINE

Strategically Paying Off Debt

Mayah stared at her credit card statements and other debt obligations with frustration knotting in her stomach. Despite her efforts to save, debt still loomed over her.

She had tried paying extra when she could, but she felt like the credit card balances barely moved as the interest charges wiped out her progress every month.

When she met Mr. Clark at the coffee shop, he could see the frustration on her face and knew she was concerned about the mountain of debt she had told him about.

As a money mentor, Mr. Clark was known for keeping it real and he decided to give Mayah a wakeup call about how to tackle debt head-on.

Mr. Clark said, "Some people are only interested in looking rich. They use all their money to buy expensive things, trying to deceive others into believing they have it going on, but in reality, they are only deceiving themselves."

With a serious look on his face, Mr. Clark said, "Self-deception is the worst kind of deceitfulness."

He looked intently at Mayah and said, "Now let me show you how to crush your debt and regain control over your money. It's time for you to implement a strategy where you are not just paying when you can, but attacking your debt with a systematic plan."

A SYSTEMATIC PLAN FOR ATTACKING DEBT

Step 1: Understand the Cost of Debt.

As Mayah handed him her credit card statements, Mr. Clark pulled out his calculator. "Let's look at the real impact of your debt."

Card #1: $9,103 at 22% interest

Card #2: $8,732 at 19% interest

Card #3: $320 at 17% interest

Added to this was:

Car Lease: $700 per month

Apartment rent: $2,500 per month

After some quick math, Mr. Clark noted, "Right now, your credit card interest alone is costing you about $2,000 a year. That's money going straight to the bank instead of building wealth for your future."

Mayah took a deep breath and exhaled. "I knew it was bad, but seeing the numbers hurts."

Mr. Clark nodded. "That's why we need to free up cash flow so you can quickly destroy this debt."

Step 2: Free Up Cash by Downsizing and Renegotiating.

Tapping on Mayah's biggest expenses—her apartment and car lease—Mr. Clark asked, "What if you moved to a smaller place?"

Mayah hesitated. "I love my apartment."

"I get that. But if you move out of your $2,500 apartment and find a less expensive apartment for around $1,800, you will save $750. This is money you could use to crush your debt."

Mayah exhaled. "I never thought about it that way."

Mr. Clark continued. "And your car lease. Have you considered renegotiating or even swapping it for a less expensive car?"

Mayah frowned. "Can you even do that?"

Mr. Clark nodded. "Some dealerships let you trade down to a lower payment. Or you could take over a used car lease for less. Just think about it. Renegotiating your $700 car lease and buying a pre-owned use car with a monthly payment of no more than $450 will save another $250."

Mayah bit her lip. "So, if I did both…I could free up nearly $1,000 a month."

Mr. Clark smiled. "Now you're thinking like a strategist."

Step 3: Plan Your Debt Payoff.

After freeing up some cash for Mayah, Mr. Clark offered her two payoff options: the Snowball Method and the Avalanche Method.

The Snowball Method focuses on paying off the smallest debt first, regardless of interest rates. This builds momentum and motivation as one debt is eliminated at a time.

The Avalanche Method, on the other hand, focuses on paying off the debt with the highest interest rate first, which saves you the most money over time.

Mayah chose the Avalanche Method—starting with her highest-interest credit card.

"With your extra $1,000 a month, you can wipe out your $9,103 balance within 9 months instead of years," Mr. Clark pointed out.

He added, "Now, let's focus on how to repay your student loans because paying off student loans efficiently requires a mix of smart budgeting and financial discipline.

He offered the following key strategies:

REPAYMENT OF STUDENT LOANS

1. Understand Your Loans.

- **The first thing you must do is identify loan types (federal vs. private), interest rates, and repayment terms.**

- **Prioritize loans with the highest interest rates first (Avalanche Method) or focus on small balances for motivation (Snowball Method), similar to strategies for repaying credit cards.**

2. *Choose the Best Repayment Plan.*

- **Federal loans: Consider income-driven repayment plans if you need lower monthly payments.**

- **Private loans: Look for refinancing options to secure a lower interest rate. Be cautious with refinancing federal loans because this could mean losing access to income-driven plans and forgiveness options.**

3. *Live Below Your Means and Avoid Lifestyle Inflation.*

- **Keep expenses low, even after getting a raise.**

- **Allocate extra income toward student loan repayment rather than unnecessary spending.**

After reviewing Mayah's situation with a $35,000 federal student loan at 5.5% interest, Mr. Clark devised a flexible approach that balanced loan repayment with other financial goals.

Writing in Mayah's notebook, he outlined the following tailored plan for her:

1. **Log into Studentaid.gov to check current repayment plan and compare income-driven repayment options.**

2. **Apply for an income-driven plan to buy time for building savings and making small extra payments of $50–$100 per month to reduce interest and shorten repayment.**

3. **Increase income, cut expenses, work on credit score, and invest alongside paying off debt.**

Mayah felt a surge of excitement. "I never realized I had this much power over my financial situation."

"That's the thing about money," Mr. Clark stated, "It's not just about working harder to make more, but it's also about making smarter moves with it."

Mayah's Next Challenge

Mayah left their meeting with a plan:

- **Find a more affordable apartment and move within the next three months.**

- **Renegotiate or trade down her car lease to free up cash.**

- **Attack her highest interest debt first using the Avalanche Method.**

- **Repay her student loans using the income-driven plan.**

As she sat in her apartment writing in her notebook, she no longer felt trapped by debt.

For the first time, she saw a way to break free from it.

The fifth step to money mastery: Live within your means.

CHAPTER TEN

The Truth about Budgeting

After a few weeks, Mayah slid into the café booth with a small smile on her face.

Mr. Clark, was glad to see Mayah. Although he was also helping other people gain control over their money, mentoring Mayah was like teaching one of his own daughters. He observed, "You look different today."

Mayah smirked. "I passed your little test."

"Did you pay yourself first?"

She nodded. "Yeah. And let me tell you—it was hard. I almost caved, but I made it work."

Mr. Clark leaned back. "Good. Now let's make it easier."

"How?"

Mr. Clark asked Mayah to pull out her notebook and start writing, "By giving every dollar a job."

He then asked, "Do you know where your money goes? You make $4,500 a month, right?"

Mayah nodded.

"And before, your paycheck would come in and then you'd spend it until it was gone, hoping there'd be something left at the end."

Mayah made a sassy face with her smile. "Pretty much."

"That's not a budget. That's winging it."

Mayah took a deep breath. "Okay, but budgets suck. I've tried. They always feel like I'm punishing myself."

"That's because you've been looking at budgeting wrong. It's not about restriction—it's about control," Mr. Clark admonished.

"Control?"

Mr. Clark nodded. "A budget isn't about saying "no" to spending. It's about telling your money where to go before it disappears."

Mayah thought about it. "So...instead of cutting things, I'm just deciding where everything goes up front?"

"Exactly. And once you have a plan, you will stop feeling guilty about spending money because you already accounted for it."

The Simple Budget Plan

Mr. Clark drew four boxes in Mayah's notebook and labelled them:

1. Pay Yourself First (10%)

2. Needs (60%)

3. Wants (20%)

4. Future Growth (10%)

Mayah tilted her head. "Wait…this is a 60/20/20 budget, right?"

Mr. Clark nodded. "A variation of it. But instead of thinking of it as rules, think of it as a framework. The goal is balance."

He pointed to the first box. "You already passed the first test—paying yourself first. That 10% is non-negotiable."

Mayah nodded. "Got it."

Pointing to the second box, Mr. Clark said, "Then, you cover your needs. Rent, food, transportation—items you literally can't live without. Try to keep this under 60% of your income."

Mayah winced. "That's gonna be tough. My rent alone eats up almost half my paycheck."

"I know. That's why we're looking at the full picture—so you can start making changes if you need to."

He then tapped the third box. "Next, we have wants: eating out, shopping, paying for Netflix—whatever makes life enjoyable—around 20%."

"So, I'm allowed to spend on fun stuff?" Mayah asked raising an eyebrow.

Mr. Clark smiled. "Of course. You just plan for it, instead of feeling guilty later."

Mayah nodded slowly. This budget plan was making sense.

Then Mr. Clark pointed to the last box. "And finally, Future Growth."

"Wait, what's the difference between this and 'paying myself first'?"

Mr. Clark smiled. "Paying yourself first is saving for security. Future growth is building wealth. This is where investing comes in."

Mayah leaned forward. "Investing? Like in stocks?"

Mr. Clark nodded affirmatively. "That's a conversation for later. First, you need to master this budget plan."

MAYAH'S NEXT CHALLENGE

Mr. Clark pushed the notebook toward Mayah. "This is your next assignment. For the next month, track where every dollar goes and fit it into these categories. No cheating."

Mayah groaned. "So, I have to write down everything?"

"You want control over your money, don't you?"

"Fine," Mayah agreed. "But if I hate it, I'm blaming you."

Mr. Clark laughed and said. "Fair deal."

Mayah glanced at the notebook, and for the first time, thought that budgeting didn't feel like a punishment.

So maybe—just maybe—this type of budgeting would actually work for her.

The sixth step to money mastery: If you spend more than you make, you will never get ahead financially.

CHAPTER ELEVEN

Spend with a Purpose

Mayah sat on her couch, scrolling through her bank transactions.

One week into her budgeting assignment, and things were...not terrible.

She had been tracking her spending—mostly. She wrote down big purchases like rent, groceries, and bills.

But the little things?

That's where it got messy.

She had forgotten to note a coffee run. Then a few days later, she realized she hadn't written down the $12 she spent on snacks at the gas station.

By the time she checked her bank account, $50 had disappeared.

And she had no idea where it went.

DEATH BY A THOUSAND SMALL PURCHASES

Mayah pulled out her notebook, in which she had been trying to track her spending.

- **Rent? Logged.**
- **Car payment? Logged.**
- **Streaming subscriptions? Logged.**

But all the small, everyday purchases? They were slipping through the cracks.

She groaned. "This is harder than I thought."

She had assumed budgeting would just mean being more aware of her spending, but knowing where her big money went wasn't the problem.

It was the small, daily decisions that were throwing everything off.

She needed a better system.

MR. CLARK'S ADVICE

The next time she met with Mr. Clark, she dropped her notebook on the table. "All right, I did it. Kind of."

Mr. Clark had a serious look on his face and asked, "Kind of?"

Mayah took a deep breath before clarifying, "I tracked the big stuff, but the small expenses kept slipping. I'd forget to write them down, and before I knew it, I had no idea where my money went."

Mr. Clark nodded. "This happens to most people. You're not used to watching your money yet. But there's an easier way."

Mayah perked up. "Easier?"

"Yes," Mr. Clark smiled. "Automation."

THE POWER OF AUTOMATIC BUDGETING

Mr. Clark pulled out his phone. "You don't need to manually track everything. Instead, use your bank's tools. Most banks let you categorize transactions automatically. Or you can use a budgeting app that tracks spending for you."

Mayah frowned. "But doesn't that take the awareness out of it?"

"Not at all. It makes things clearer. Instead of you guessing where your money went, an app or your bank's tracker will show you in real time. No forgetting, no surprises."

Mayah considered this. "So, I just check the app every few days instead of writing it all down?"

"Exactly," Mr. Clark nodded. And while you're at it, automate paying yourself first too. Set up an automatic transfer so you don't even have to think about it."

Mayah leaned back. "So instead of budgeting being work, it just runs in the background?"

Mr. Clark smiled. "Now you're getting it. Tracking your spending will help you spend with a purpose."

MAYAH'S NEXT CHALLENGE

Mr. Clark asked for Mayah notebook and wrote, "Set up automation with categories in your bank app. Also set up automatic savings transfers and a budgeting app if you need it."

Mayah exhaled. "All right. Let's see if technology can do this better than I can."

"It will," Mr. Clark laughed. "But don't get too comfortable yet—the real test is what you do with the extra money."

Mayah raised an eyebrow. "Extra money?"

"Yep. Budgeting isn't just about tracking. It's about making room for growth. When you learn to eliminate wasteful spending, you will keep more of your money, and that's where your future wealth comes in." The money you save will start making more money for you through the power of compound interest.

The seventh step to money mastery:
Be prepared for the unexpected.

CHAPTER TWELVE

Save for a Rainy Day

Mayah stared at her bank app, watching as her spending tracker finally made sense.

Everything was automated now—her bills, savings, and even her spending categories. She wasn't scrambling to write down purchases or wondering where her money went.

For the first time in her adult life, she felt in control of her money.

But then Mr. Clark threw her a curveball. "You need an emergency fund."

Mayah frowned. "Isn't that what my savings are for?"

Mr. Clark shook his head "no" and said, "Paying yourself first is savings for future goals. When you save for a rainy day it is insurance against life uncertainties."

"Look!" he continued. "Unexpected expenses, such as a loss of employment, expensive medical bills, past-due household bills, past-due mortgage or rent payments, expensive automobile repairs, broken household appliances, and other unknown expenses can strain even the most carefully managed budget.

"If you are financially unprepared to protect yourself because you have no emergency fund, life will force you into making money moves you do not want to make.

"With an emergency fund, you wouldn't have to worry about unexpected financial expenses because you would have the resources to handle them without going into debt.

"Unlike a regular savings account, which may be used for vacations or major purchases, an emergency fund is strictly for unplanned expenses."

WHY HAVE AN EMERGENCY FUND?

Mr. Clark leaned back. "Think about the last time an unexpected expense hit you."

Mayah thought about her car battery dying. "Yeah, I had to use my checking account. Almost pulled from savings."

"And what if it had been bigger?" Mr. Clark asked. "A medical bill? A job loss? A sudden move?"

Mayah exhaled. "I'd be ruined."

"Exactly. An emergency fund is what keeps you from going into debt when life throws you a curveball."

HOW MUCH IS ENOUGH?

Mr. Clark held up six fingers, explaining, "Six to ten months of expenses. That's the goal."

"That's a lot of money," Mayah noted with widened eyes.

Mr. Clark said, "When it comes to how much to save in your emergency fund, you will use this approach to calculate your target fund. He then explained the following strategies to determine how much to save in an emergency fund.

Step 1: List your essential monthly expenses, including:

    Rent/Mortgage

    Utilities (electricity, gas, water, internet, etc.)

    Groceries

    Transportation

    Insurance (car, health, home)

    Debt payments

    Other critical expenses

Step 2: Multiply this amount by 6 to 10 months to determine your emergency fund goal.

For example:

- **Let's say your monthly essential expenses are: $3,000.**

- **For a six-month emergency fund, you will need to save: $18,000.**

- **For a ten-month emergency fund, you will need to save: $30,000.**

Mr. Clark cautioned, "Someone might be thinking, with all the debt I am currently paying, I can't afford to save that much. Remember, this is your emergency fund. Do not let debt stop you from saving something.

"If saving six to ten months of expenses seem overwhelming, start small with a 'starter emergency fund' of $1,000–$3,000. Make consistent contributions like $100 from every paycheck. Trust me, even this small amount will start to add up over time.

"Once you reach your goal, expand it to one month of expenses, then three months, and so on.

Also, look for ways to cut unnecessary expenses like subscriptions, dining out, shopping, etc."

Mayah asked, "What if I need to use it before it's fully funded?"

"That's okay!" Mr. Clark responded. "The purpose of an emergency fund is to be used for real emergencies. Just rebuild it once you're financially stable again."

Mayah nodded slowly and said, "This emergency fund plan seems doable, but where should I keep it?"

Mr. Clark looked and Mayah and said, "Here is the rest of the plan."

BEST PLACES TO KEEP YOUR EMERGENCY FUND

1. A High-Yield Savings Account (HYSA) is one of the best places to store your emergency fund. These accounts offer higher interest rates than traditional savings accounts while keeping your money accessible.

2. A Money Market Account (MMA) is another good place to store your emergency fund because it combines the benefits of savings and checking accounts. Although it has a slightly higher

interest rate than HYSAs, it may require a higher minimum balance with limited withdrawals per month.

3. A Certificate of Deposit (CD) might look like a good place to store your emergency fund, but it is not really. This kind of account locks your money away for a set period of time, like six months, one year, three years, or more. This kind of account offers a fixed interest rate, but has withdrawal penalties if you need to get your money for an emergency before the maturity date.

4. Another good place to store your emergency fund is at home. Keeping a small amount of cash at home for emergencies like natural disasters, power outages, or banking system failures can give you immediate access to the money when time is of the essence.

MAYAH'S NEXT CHALLENGE

Mr. Clark smiled and said, "Set up a separate account, transfer a set amount every paycheck, and let it grow. And, of course, don't forget to automate."

Mayah exhaled. "All right. Emergency fund, here I come."

"Good," Mr. Clark said. "Because once you have a safety net, we move to the real money mastery game of investing."

The eighth step to money mastery: Make your money make money.

CHAPTER THIRTEEN

The Money Multiplier

Mayah sat across from Mr. Clark with her bank app open. A small smile was creeping across her face as she claimed, "I did it." She slid her phone toward him.

Mr. Clark glanced at the screen: "1,000 in savings."

He nodded approvingly. "Good! That's your safety net."

Mayah took a deep breath and exhaled. "I feel secure. Like if something went wrong, I wouldn't be in full panic mode."

"That's the point. Now, let's talk about putting your money to work."

Mayah, who is now opened to learning money mastery, asked, "You mean investing?"

"Yes," Mr. Clark responded. "And before you ask—no, investing isn't just for rich people. It's how people become rich." He offered the following information.

"Imagine planting a small seed in your backyard. At first, it's just a tiny sprout, barely noticeable. But with time, care, and patience, it grows into a strong tree, bearing fruit year after year. Investing works the same way with small actions today that can grow into lasting wealth over time.

"Many people believe investing is complicated, risky, or only for the wealthy. The truth? Investing is one of the most powerful tools for financial growth, and anyone can start, no matter what their income level. The key is to understand how it works and to develop a long-term mindset.

"At its core, investing is about making your money work for you. Instead of just spending, you put your money into assets like stocks, bonds, index funds, or real estate that grows in value over time. The earlier you start, the more you can benefit from the power of compound interest, where your earning generate even more earnings, creating exponential growth."

Mayah listened intently to everything Mr. Clark said.

THE POWER OF COMPOUND INTEREST

Mr. Clark asked Mayah for her notebook and wrote two numbers:

$10,000 in cash

$10,000 invested

He pointed to the first number. "If you save this amount and leave this in a regular savings account, it will earn almost nothing. After 20 years, it will only be a few thousand dollars more at best."

"Makes sense," Mayah said as she studied Mr. Clark.

Then he pointed to the second number. "But if you invest it and earn an average of 8%–10% a year—which is what the stock market has done historically—after 20 years, that same money becomes..." and he quickly scribbled: $46,610.

Mayah's eyes popped wide. "Wait...what?"

"That's the power of compound interest," Mr. Clark noted with a grin. "Your money makes money. Then that money makes more money. And over time, it snowballs."

THE REAL COST OF WAITING

Mayah crossed her arms. "Okay, but what if I don't have $10,000 sitting around?"

Mr. Clark smiled. "Let's say you start with just $100 a month." He ran the numbers: "After 30 years, at an 8% return, you will have $146,000 in wealth."

Mayah's jaw dropped.

Mr. Clark leaned forward. "And if you waited 10 years to start? You'd have only $66,000."

Mayah's stomach sank. "So...the longer I wait, the more I lose?"

"Time is your biggest asset. The earlier you start, the less you have to invest to get the same results."

Mayah exhaled. "Okay. I get it. I need to start now."

"Exactly."

MAYAH'S NEXT CHALLENGE

Mr. Clark passed Mayah notebook back to her and said, Now that you understand why investing matters, the next step is understanding where to invest. "Stocks, index funds, real estate—you need to know your options."

Mayah said, "Let's do it."

The ninth step to money mastery:
Your money will grow when you invest it wisely.

CHAPTER FOURTEEN

The Simple Path to Wealth

"All right," Mayah said as she sipped her coffee during her meeting with Mr. Clark. "I get that investing early is key. But where do I even put my money? Stocks? Crypto? Real estate?"

Mr. Clark laughed. "We'll get to all that. But first, let's start with the simplest, most effective investment for beginners—index funds."

"Why index funds?"

"Because they make you money without you needing to be a stock-picking genius."

WHAT IS AN INDEX FUND?

Mr. Clark pulled out his phone and typed something. Then he slid the device over to Mayah.

On the phone was a chart of the S&P 500's growth over the last 30 years. Mayah traced the upward trend with her finger. "Okay…what am I looking at?"

Mr. Clark explained. "The S&P 500 is a collection of the 500 biggest companies in the United States. Instead of trying to pick individual stocks, an index fund invests in all 500 at once."

Mayah blinked. "So, instead of betting on one company, I'm betting on...all of them?"

Mr. Clark responded. "Exactly. And because the stock market tends to go up over time, your money grows with it."

WHY INDEX FUNDS WORK

Mr. Clark took back his phone and pulled up another number. "The average return of the S&P 500 over the last century was about 8–10% per year."

Mayah frowned. "That doesn't sound like much."

"It is when you let compound interest do its thing. Remember what I told you before."

Then he asked Mayah to pull out her notebook and in it he wrote:

$500/month in an index fund

8% average annual return

30 years of investment

Likely return of $745,000

Mayah's mouth fell open. "No way."

But the lessons she had been learning from Mr. Clark all came back to her, and the information did make sense.

Mr. Clark said, "And you don't have to pick stocks, time the market, or stress about crashes. Just keep investing, and the market will do the heavy lifting."

THE SET-AND-FORGET STRATEGY

Mayah exhaled. "So, I just...put my money in and leave it?"

Mr. Clark responded. "Exactly. It's called dollar-cost averaging. You invest the same amount every month—whether the market is up or down. Over time, you smooth out the ups and downs and keep growing your wealth."

Mayah tapped her chin. "So...where do I buy an index fund?"

"Now you're asking the right questions." Instead of giving Mayah another challenge, he asked her to take out her phone so that he could show her how to set up an index fund. There are five basic steps," Mr. Clark noted.

Step 1: Open a brokerage account.

Step 2: Choose your index fund.

Step 3: Deposit money into your account.

Step 4: Buy the index fund shares.

Step 5: Set up automatic investments.

Step 1: Open a Brokerage Account.

Mr. Clark pointed at the screen. "First, you need a brokerage account. This is like a bank account, but for investing."

Mayah scrolled through a list. "Which one should I pick?"

"Go with a trusted brokerage like Vanguard, Fidelity, or Charles Schwab. They all offer low-cost index funds." Mr. Clark suggested that Mayah go with Fidelity (https://www.fidelity.com).

Mayah tapped the icon and created an account, filling in her personal information.

Step 2: Choose Your Index Fund.

"Now, you need to pick your index fund," Mr. Clark said. "There are a few great options." For example:

- **S&P 500 Index Fund (VFIAX, FXAIX, SWPPX): Invests in 500 top U.S. companies.**

- **Total Stock Market Index Fund (VTSAX, FSKAX, SWTSX): Covers the entire U.S. stock market.**

- **International Index Fund (VTIAX, FZILX, SWISX): Includes companies from around the world.**

Mayah asked, "Which one is best?"

Mr. Clark smiled. "If you want to keep it simple, go with an S&P 500 fund. If you want everything, go with a Total Stock Market fund."

Mayah tapped the FXAIX (Fidelity® 500 Index Fund). "All right, I like the sound of this one."

Step 3: Deposit Money into Your Account.

Mr. Clark said, "Now you need to fund your account, that is, transfer some money from your bank."

Mayah hesitated. "How much should I start with?"

"Whatever you're comfortable with. Even $100 is a good start."

Mayah typed in $200, and hit the transfer button. "All right, the money is on the way."

Step 4: Buy the Index Fund Shares.

Mr. Clark pointed to the screen. "Now, find the fund and hit 'Buy.'"

Mayah entered FXAIX, set the amount to invest, and clicked "Confirm."

Mr. Clark clapped his hands. "And just like that, you own a piece of 500 of the biggest companies in the United States. Welcome to the investor's club!"

Step 5: Set Up Automatic Investments.

Mr. Clark continued, "Now, let's make this easy. Set up an automatic monthly investment—$50, $100, or whatever you can afford."

Mayah entered $100 per month for automatic investing. "All right, it's set."

"Congrats. You're officially an investor."

Mayah let out a deep breath while staring at the confirmation screen. "That was easier than I thought it would be."

Mr. Clark laughed. "Investing isn't complicated. Like I said, 'The hard part is sticking with it and not panicking when the market dips.'"

Now that you have mastered index funds, it's time to talk about the next level of investing—real estate and passive income.

Mayah looked at Mr. Clark with a big smile on her face because she had the feeling of something she have never had before—control over her financial future.

The tenth step to money mastery: Make your money work for you through a multitude of investments.

CHAPTER FIFTEEN

Building Multiple Streams of Income

Mayah sat across from Mr. Clark with fresh excitement in her eyes.

"Okay," she said, "Now that I've set up my index fund investment, I want to know how to make extra money. I keep hearing about side hustles and real estate. What is that all about?"

Mr. Clark smiled. "Now you're thinking like an investor. The goal isn't just to save and invest; it's to build multiple streams of income. That way, if one steam slows down, the others will keep you afloat."

Mayah was all in. "Okay, let's start with side hustles. What's worth my time?"

THE POWER OF A SIDE HUSTLE

Leaning back, Mr. Clark explained, "A side hustle does two things: it brings in extra cash and it gives you a skill that could turn into something bigger."

"Like what?"

"It depends on what you're good at. Some people freelance as a photographer, blogger, personal trainer, housekeeper, graphic designer, or consultant. Others start online businesses flipping items; someone can start a small business offering childcare services, tutoring services, or digital product sales. The key is to leverage your skills."

Mayah frowned. "What if I don't have any marketable skills?"

Mr. Clark laughed. "That's the biggest lie people tell themselves. Everyone has something people will pay for. The trick is figuring it out and finding something you already know and enjoy. Let's brainstorm."

FINDING THE RIGHT SIDE HUSTLE

Mr. Clark asked Mayah to give him her notebook. "Let's break it down. What do you enjoy doing?"

Mayah hesitated. "I like organizing things. I'm good at making schedules, planning, keeping things on track."

"That's a skill. Virtual assistants make $20–$50 an hour doing exactly that."

Mayah's eyes widened. "Wait, people pay for that?"

Mr. Clark nodded "yes." "Businesses, entrepreneurs, even busy professionals will all pay. You could start small, build up clients, and eventually scale it into a full-time business if you wanted."

"Okay…I never thought of it that way."

Mr. Clark chuckled. "And that's just one option. The key is to start testing ideas. Select a skill, offer a service, and see what happens."

THE THREE PATHS TO INCOME

Mr. Clark told Mayah that there are three paths to income. In her notebook, he wrote down the three ways and their definitions:

1. Earned Income: Money from your job.

2. Business Income: Money from a side hustle or business.

3. Passive Income: Money that comes in even when you're not actively working.

"You rely on earned income right now. That's fine, but it has a limit because there are only so many hours in a day. If you want to build wealth faster, you need to create business income or passive income."

A STORY ABOUT TWO FRIENDS

Mr. Clark leaned back in his chair. "Let me tell you about two men I once knew who worked together at the same company. Let's call them Allen and Marcus.

"Allen worked a solid 9-to-5 job. He was responsible, saved a little, and hoped for a raise every few years.

"Marcus, on the other hand, also had a solid job, but instead of waiting for a raise, he started a small business on the side. It wasn't much at first, just a weekend gig fixing up old furniture and selling it online.

"But over time, that little side business started bringing in more and more money. Eventually, he was making just as much from his side hustle as he was from his job.

"One day, their company started laying off people. Allen panicked because his only source of income was gone. But Marcus? He simply expanded his business and never had to worry."

Mayah nodded slowly. "So, you're saying…having a side hustle or passive income gives you financial security?"

"Exactly," said Mr. Clark. "Wealthy people don't depend on one paycheck. They build multiple streams of income so money flows to them in different ways."

Mayah slowly smiled. "So instead of just working harder at my job, I should focus on creating new income streams?"

"Exactly," Mr. Clark repeated. "The goal is to have money coming in from multiple sources, so you're never completely dependent on just one."

Mayah flashed a wide smile. "I will use my marketing and planning skills to start an event planning side hustle." I will build this side hustle into a thriving business to grow my income, and then funnel that money into other investments.

"Now you're getting it," Mr. Clark smiled. "Because once you start making money work for you, wealth will not be just a dream—it will be an inevitability."

The eleventh step to money mastery: Pool money to build shared wealth.

CHAPTER SIXTEEN

Producing Income for the Future

Mr. Clark took a sip of his coffee, then said, "Now that you have extra money coming in from your side hustle, the real fun begins because I will teach you how to invest in real estate as an income-producing asset."

Mayah perked up. "I've always been curious about rental properties. But don't you need a ton of money?"

Mr. Clark shook his head "no." "Not necessarily. There are ways to get started without six figures in the bank."

Mayah leaned closer. "Like what?"

Mr. Clark asked Mayah for her notebook and started writing the following list.

HOW TO GET INTO REAL ESTATE WITHOUT A FORTUNE

- **House Hacking:** Buy a duplex; live in one unit; rent out the other. The rent covers your mortgage.

- **Low Down-Payment Loans:** Federal Housing

Administration (FHA) loans allow you to buy a house with as little as 3.5% down.

- **Partnerships:** Team up with someone who has money but no time, and then split the profits.

- **REITs (Real Estate Investment):** Invest in real estate without owning property by buying shares of a REIT.

Mayah's mind was racing. "So, you don't need to be rich—you just need the right strategy?"

Mr. Clark nodded "yes." "Exactly. Using the income from your side hustle to fund your first property is the best way to get started, but I want you to think BIG with an entrepreneurial mindset."

"What do you mean by an *entrepreneurial mindset?*"

Mr. Clark answered, "It is a particular way of thinking that allows you to identify and take advantage of opportunities that are disguised as problems or challenges.

"When it comes to investing in real estate, you cannot be ruled by fear, greed, emotions, or the opinions of others. You must develop a mindset where nothing bothers you, and you are always thinking strategically about how to reach your full money-making potential.

"Most people fail not because of bad investments, but because they let fear control their decisions.

"If you can master your fears, greed, emotions, and the opinion of others, you'll master money."

Mayah stared at Mr. Clark without saying a word, but she knew he was speaking to her specifically, especially on the topic of fear and the emotional side of money."

Since Mr. Clark had to leave for a business meeting, they agreed to meet next week to work on a real estate investment plan.

Mayah took a deep breath and exhaled because she had a lot to think about.

THE IDEA IS BORN

The next day, Mayah was having dinner with her three closest friends: Erica, Aaliyah, and Ebony. They were all doing well financially, and wanted to take their wealth-building to the next level.

Mayah shared with the group how her investments were growing, and how she wanted to build long-term wealth through real estate.

Ebony chimed in. "I've been thinking about real estate also, but I don't have enough for a down payment."

Aaliyah asked the group, "What if we invest together?"

Ebony quickly queried, "You mean like buy a property as a group?"

They looked at each other with sparkling eyes, and suddenly, the idea of pooling their money to build shared wealth through real estate began to feel real.

Mayah invited her three friends to go with her to meet with Mr. Clark, her money mentor, who would help guide them, step by step, on their real estate investment journey.

Mayah called Mr. Clark to tell him about her plan to pool money with her three friends to invest in real estate. She asked Mr. Clark if he would meet with the group and guide them through the process of residential property investment, and he quickly agreed.

GUIDANCE ON RESIDENTIAL PROPERTY INVESTMENT

Mr. Clark met Mayah and her three friends at the coffee shop to discuss their real estate investment goals. He laid out the following plans.

1. Understanding the Investment Plan

First he asked them:

- **What type of residential property do you want to invest in (single-family, duplex, or multi-unit)?**
- **What is your investment horizon (short-term rental, long-term buy-and-hold, fix-and-flip)?**
- **How much can each of you contribute?**

Mr. Clark emphasized the need for a written business plan outlining:

- **The investment strategy (rental income, flipping, or appreciation).**
- **The roles and responsibilities of each member.**
- **The exit strategy if someone wants to leave.**

Before they could give an answer, Mr. Clark, looking at them seriously, said, "Friendships and money can get messy, so treat this like a business from Day One."

Mayah, Erica, Aaliyah, and Ebony all agreed that their initial goal was "rental income." They explained, "We want to buy a duplex property and collect rent."

"Good," Mr. Clark nodded approvingly. "Long-term wealth is built on cash flow. Now, how much money are we working with?"

Erica opened a spreadsheet. "We've each saved around $15,000. That's $60,000 total."

Mr. Clark said, "That's a solid start. With a 20% down payment, that means you can afford a property up to around $300,000."

Now, have you considered financing?

The group had a puzzled look on each of their faces.

Mr. Clark said, "Don't worry, I will teach you everything you need to know about financing and ownership structure.

2. Setting Up the Business Structure

Aaliyah offered, "We were thinking of just buying together, but we heard an LLC might be better."

Mr. Clark smiled. "Absolutely. An LLC protects your personal assets and makes things cleaner for taxes. More importantly, you need an operating agreement that spells out who owns what, how profits are split, and what happens if someone wants out."

He pulled out a sample Operating Agreement and slid it across the table.

Mr. Clark asked the group to go through the following Operating Agreement and make sure it worked for them because they wouldn't want any surprises later.

Operating Agreement for Setting Up an LLC

Step 1: Select a Business Name—one that is professional, easy to remember, and reflects their investment goals. Some examples:

- FirstGen Real Estate Partners
- Infinity Legacy Investments
- 4Keys Investment Group

Step 2: Go to LegalZoon.com or another online site to create your LLC. This will not only help you register the business name with the Internal Revenue Service (IRS), but also help with registering in your state and help with drafting an Operating Agreement (how profits/losses are shared, decision-making, dispute resolution).

Step 3: Once your LLC is created and you receive all legal documents, open a joint business bank account. This will ensure you do not mix business funds with personal funds.

Step 4: Go to a United Parcel Service (UPS) site and obtain a business address mailbox until you can afford a permanent business location.

3. Property Research and Analysis

Mayah said, "So how do we find the right property?"

Mr. Clark looked at the group and said, "Great question." He then offered these two steps.

1. **You must look at rental demand. You want a place where people need housing, like near colleges, business districts, or hospitals.**
2. **You must run the 1% rule. If a $250,000 property can rent for at least $2,500 a month, it's worth considering.**

He opened online platforms like Zillow and Realtor.com on his tablet to shortlist properties, and said, "Here's an example. This duplex is in a growing neighborhood. The asking price is $280,000."

The group drew closer to his screen, excited.

Ebony commented, "If we put 20% down, that's $56,000. Perfect."

Mayah added, "And if we rent both units for $1,400 each, we'll make $2,800 per month!"

The group agreed in unison, "That works for us."

Mr. Clark smiled. He let them know that next they would need to conduct property visits and check for the following:

- **Condition of the roof, plumbing, and foundation.**
- **Neighborhood appreciation trends.**
- **Proximity to schools, transportation, and job hubs.**

The preceding checks are all part of the due diligence process of identifying and analyzing properties before making an offer.

4. Financing and Making an Offer

Erica and Aaliyah said, "We're still unsure how to get a loan as a group."

Mr. Clark replied, "You have two options. 1) You can take out a commercial loan under the LLC. Or 2) You can all co-sign a mortgage together. The second option ties your credit scores together, so be careful."

Mayah asked, "What about negotiating the price?"

"Always negotiate," Mr. Clark quickly answered. "You'd be surprised how often sellers come down in price. Make a lower offer and let your real estate agent push for better terms. Maybe the seller will cover the closing costs or throw in appliances."

Mr. Clark told the group that he would introduce them to his mastermind team to help them navigate their path to success. His mastermind team consisted of:

- **Dominique, his real estate agent, who specializes in investment properties.**
- **Alexandra, his mortgage broker, can help with exploring group financing options.**
- **Michelle, his attorney, who will ensure a smooth closing.**
- **Kailah, his banker, who can help set up their business account.**

- **Rashawnda, his accountant, who can help set up their bookkeeping.**

- **Mercedes, his tax advisor, who can help with taxes.**

He advised the group to work with:

- **The mortgage broker to get pre-approved for a mortgage.**

- **The real estate agent to negotiate purchase price and closing costs as well as to hire an inspector before making an offer.**

- **The attorney for any legal matters.**

Mr. Clark also told them that the other members of the mastermind would come into play as they are needed.

5. *Managing the Investment*

Mayah asked, "After we buy a property, what's next?"

"Tenant screening is key," Mr. Clark noted. "Irresponsible tenants cost you money because, if they are late in paying or don't pay rent, you will need to pay it. Also, any damage they may cause will come out of your pocket. This is the reason you want to run background checks, verify employment, and call previous landlords to make sure you are getting renters who are responsible and trustworthy. Also, set aside money in a separate rental bank account for maintenance because things break, and you need a financial cushion."

Ebony asked, "Should we hire a property manager?"

"It depends. If you don't want late-night calls about broken toilets, a management company can handle it for 8–12% of the rent. Otherwise, you manage it yourself and save that money."

6. Planning for Future Growth

Aaliyah asked, "Once we get this property up and running, how do we scale?"

"Leverage," Mr. Clark replied. "Once you build equity in this property, you can borrow against it to buy another one. You build a portfolio by using the value of what you own to acquire more."

Mayah, taking furious notes, looked up with a determined expression. "So, we're not just buying a property, we're building wealth?"

Mr. Clark smiled and gave a familiar answer. "Exactly. And it starts with this first investment. Are you ready?"

The group exchanged glances, then nodded in agreement. "We're all in," they said in chorus.

Mr. Clark wrapped up the meeting, "Okay, we will meet again once you have found a property and are ready to close the deal."

CLOSING THE REAL ESTATE DEAL

A few weeks later, Mayah and her friends gathered in a sleek conference room at the real estate attorney's office. The walls were lined with framed documents, and a large table in the center of the room was covered in paperwork. The group's real estate agent, Dominique, sat at one end, while Mr. Clark observed from the side, periodically nodding approvingly.

Step 1. Reviewing the Final Numbers

Dominique said, "All right, team. You've done the hard work—now let's go over the final numbers before signing."

She pulled out the Closing Disclosure and slid copies to each of the investors.

>Purchase price: $275,000
>
>Down payment (20%): $55,000
>
>Loan amount: $220,000
>
>Closing costs (3%): $8,250
>
>Total cash needed: $63,250 (covered by their $60,000 savings + an additional $3,250 from rental reserves)

Mr. Clark commented, "Everything looks good here. Remember, closing costs are just part of the deal. The key is ensuring you have reserves for the first few months of expenses."

Mayah, flipping through the papers, looked up. "What about the LLC structure—does the mortgage go under our personal names or the company's name?"

Dominique answered, "The lender approved the LLC structure, so the loan is in the company's name. That protects your personal credit, but you all had to personally guarantee it since it's your first investment."

"That's normal," Mr. Clark explained. "Over time, as you build a track record, lenders will approve loans just in the LLC's name, no guarantees needed."

Step 2. Signing the Mortgage and Ownership Papers

Michelle, the attorney, entered, smiling. "All right, ladies. You're officially about to become property owners. Here are the key documents."

- **LLC Operating Agreement: Clarifies each person's ownership percentage (25% each) and responsibilities.**
- **Mortgage Agreement: Outlines loan terms (5.5% fixed interest, 30-year term).**
- **Deed of Ownership: Officially transfers the property to their LLC.**

One by one, Mayah, Erica, Aaliyah, and Ebony signed the documents. The weight of the moment settled in, and they all realized this wasn't just paperwork. This was ownership.

Mr. Clark, watching proudly, leaned in. "How does it feel?"

Mayah grinned. "Like we're stepping into a new level of wealth."

Step 3. Planning the First Steps as Landlords

They walked out of the office, keys in hand, and Mr. Clark regathered them at a nearby coffee shop. "All right, congratulations! Now the real work begins. What's your first move?"

Aaliyah responded, "We need to get the units rent-ready. We already have an inspection report, so we know what needs fixing."

Mayah pulled out her notebook. "We should also finalize our tenant screening process with background checks, income verification, and rental history."

Mr. Clark said, "Yes, and don't forget pricing strategy. Research what similar units rent for and stay competitive."

"As for property management," Ebony noted, "We agreed to self-manage at first to save money."

Mr. Clark said, "That's fine, but set clear responsibilities now. Who will handle maintenance calls? Who will collect the rent? Create a system so things run smoothly."

Step 4. Setting the Foundation for Future Investments

Mayah asked Mr. Clark, "How soon can we use this property to buy another?"

Mr. Clark laughed, then cautioned, "Patience. Focus on making this first one successful. In a year or two, once you've built equity and proven rental income, you can refinance and use that cash for another down payment. That's how you grow your wealth."

Mayah looked around the table at her friends, who are now her business partners, and said, "Just a few months ago, we were only dreaming of wealth. Now, we have taken the first major step to acquire wealth."

Mr. Clark raised his coffee mug in a toast, "Welcome to the world of real estate investing. This is just the beginning."

Mayah stared at her notes, filled with creative ideas and real estate strategies. For the first time, she saw a clear path to long-term wealth and financial independence.

The group clinked their cups together and declared themselves partners in successful investment.

The twelveth step to money mastery: If you want to be rich, never stop Learning about money.

CHAPTER SEVENTEEN

Money Mastery Reflection

Mayah sat alone in her apartment with her money mastery notebook in front of her, filled with notes from her journey.

She flipped back to the first page, where she had scribbled her frustrations months ago:

"I make good money, but I feel broke."

"Debt is weighing heavily on my mind and preventing me from moving forward."

"I stress over small expenses, but never question the big ones."

"I'm stuck. I need a way out."

She smiled and thought to herself how far she had come.

FROM SURVIVAL TO STABILITY

She thought about the nights she had spent staring at her bank account, wondering where her money had gone. The moment of shock when she finally tracked her expenses and saw the truth.

She had cried that night, not out of hopelessness, but out of the realization that she was working to *look* rich, instead of learning how to *be* rich.

She had tried to fix her financial situation on her own, cutting back on spending, making small changes. These strategies helped, but they weren't enough.

Then she met Mr. Clark, and that was when her mindset shifted.

THE MINDSET SHIFT

Mr. Clark hadn't just taught her about money—he had changed the way she thought about it.

PAY YOURSELF FIRST

Mr. Clark said, "Before you pay a single bill, before you spend a dime, set aside at least 10% of your income for yourself. Treat it like a bill that is non-negotiable. Money should work for you, not the other way around."

He also noted, "Wealth isn't about how much you make—it's about how much you keep and grow."

At first, she had resisted his thinking. She had been skeptical. But when she started using his money mastery lessons, her financial situation began to change.

THE BREAKTHROUGHS

On her money mastery journey, Mayah had numerous breakthroughs that helped her become a money master, such as:

- **Creating a plan to eliminate debt strategically.**
- **Building her first budget—not one that restricted her, but one that gave her control.**
- **Saving her first $1,000—then watched it grow into an emergency fund.**
- **Learning how to spend with a purpose and live within her means.**
- **Investing in index funds, and starting a side hustle, and even buying her first rental property.**

BEYOND MONEY—THE BIGGER PICTURE

Now, as Mayah looked at her life, she realized wealth isn't just about numbers on a screen. For her, wealth is about:

- **Freedom—knowing that she has choices.**
- **Legacy—building something that would last beyond her.**
- **Purpose—using what she had learned to help others avoid the financial struggles she once faced.**

MAYAH'S FINAL THOUGHT

She picked up her pen and wrote one final thought in her notebook:

> "Financial freedom isn't about having millions. It's about having control over my money and making my money work for me. It's about choices. It's about knowing that no matter what happens, I will be okay—because I built this life with intention."

She closed her notebook and grinned.

She wasn't just building wealth anymore—she was lighting the path for others, proving that transformation is possible for anyone bold enough to believe and brave enough to begin rewriting their story of success with money.

ABOUT THE AUTHOR

ANANIAH CLARK was born into a low-income, working-class family dependent on government assistance to make ends meet. Despite his upbringing, he refused to see himself as poor, and he understood from the very beginning that extremely hard work would be needed to manifest his goal of overcoming his financial worries and fears.

In his twenties, Ananiah landed a good-paying job, but like most young adults, he made plenty of financial mistakes.

By age 30, he was making six figures, but he was also drowning in $32,000 of credit card debt, a luxury car loan he could not afford, zero savings, and no investments to show for his hard work.

The wake-up call came when he lost his job during an economic downturn. With no emergency fund, he couldn't even afford his rent, and after a month with no money coming in from a lack of work, he was completely broke.

This humiliation changed him forever, and he spent the next three years educating himself by reading books about money, talking to financially successful people, and learning the principles of wealth-building.

Ananiah obtained another job with a large bank making good money, but this time, he followed three rules:

1. **Pay yourself first by automatically saving 10% to 20% of every paycheck.**
2. **Live below your means with no unnecessary spending.**
3. **Invest wisely in index funds and income-producing assets like real estate and/or rental properties.**

By his mid-thirties, Ananiah had turned around his finances by paying off all his debt, building an emergency fund, investing in an index fund, investing in rental properties, and maxing out his retirement account at work.

By age 40, Ananiah was financially independent. He had multiple rental properties, a growing investment portfolio, and a thriving side business in which his money was working to make more money for him.

After seeing his younger co-workers making the same money mistakes he once made, he decided to teach them how to break free from debt, save with purpose, spend with purpose, invest wisely, and build a financial future they could be proud of. As word spread about his knowledge, people started coming to him for money management advice.

By age 50, "Mr. Clark," as he became known to his younger clientele, had become the "money mentor," helping countless people of every age transform their finances using the simple, timeless money principles that had changed his life.

He is the co-founder of PUSH To Be Great Empowerment Center located in Charlotte, North Carolina, where he educates, equips, and empowers people to reach their full potential by prioritizing and utilizing successful habits.

As an independent preacher, teacher, spiritual advisor, life coach, financial coach, author, businessman, entrepreneur, and money mentor, Ananiah is committed to enlightening people's beliefs, choices, and mindsets about their life and financial freedom.

He is considered an expert in the areas of economic empowerment, community development, spiritual development, and life skills management.

He is the published author of the book *7 Spiritual Laws of Money*. He is also the author of two upcoming books, *The Money Mentor—A Man's Guide to Money Mastery*, scheduled for release in the fall of 2025, and *You Can Do It—The Roadmap to Financial Freedom*, scheduled for release in 2026.

He lives with his wife, Berdetta, in Charlotte, North Carolina, and together, they have four children: Zyale, Devin, Iyanah, and Keyanla. They also have a daughter-in-love, Mica, and four grandchildren: Zyaire, Jai, Aarionna, and Marlei.

Made in the USA
Middletown, DE
22 June 2025

77348169R00086